For Lucy, with love — *R.R.*

For Big Zed and Az Buzz. With big love from Little Zed xx — *Z.H.*

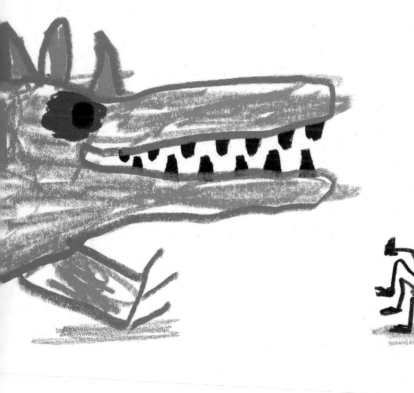

**Books for Kids From the
American Psychological Association**

First published in 2022 by Andersen Press Ltd. Original version text copyright © 2022 Rachel Rooney, illustrations copyright © 2022 Zehra Hicks.

Adapted version copyright © 2023 by Magination Press, an imprint of the American Psychological Association. All rights reserved. Except as permitted under the United States Copyright Act of 1976, no part of this publication may be reproduced or distributed in any form or by any means, or stored in a database or retrieval system, without the prior written permission of the publisher.

Magination Press is a registered trademark of the American Psychological Association.

Order books at maginationpress.org, or call 1-800-374-2721.

Cataloguing-in-Publication is available at the Library of Congress.

ISBN: 978-1-4338-4192-7

Printed in China

10 9 8 7 6 5 4 3 2 1

# The FEARS you Fear

BY RACHEL ROONEY    ILLUSTRATED BY ZEHRA HICKS

MAGINATION PRESS · AMERICAN PSYCHOLOGICAL ASSOCIATION · WASHINGTON, D.C.

A Fear is a frightening thing with legs.

Or wings.

It's large... or small.

The thing you fear, others may love.

It's different for us all.

You might meet a
Fear in a circus ring...

a fair...

or swimming pool.

It might say Hi when you wave goodbye on your very first day at school.

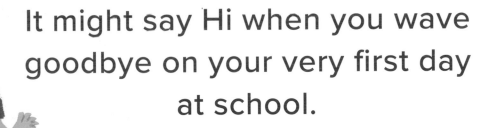

Maybe it's found at parties...

Or it sits in a dentist's chair.

Perhaps it only pesters you when no one else is there.

It might be ever so quiet...
and creep like shadows do.

It might be loud...

WHIZZ!

BANG!

Or jump out shouting...

A Fear can live in a storybook.

It can be something real.

Whatever your Fear, it's sure to be a feeling that you feel.

A Fear will give you the shivers.
A Fear will make you shake.
You'll get goosebumps.
Your heart thump-thumps.
It keeps you wide awake.

But...

You might fight your Fear and win on days you're being brave.

Or find a way to train your Fear
and teach it to behave.

Maybe you are mistaken
then you get a nice
surprise...

when you discover the feeling

is Excitement in disguise.

A Fear can be quite helpful if it warns of danger ahead.

Plugs and wires...

very hot fires...

sharp knives slicing bread.

Beeping cars on busy roads,

cliffs and
stormy
seas.

Germs that are invisible which make
you cough and sneeze.

Everyone has met a Fear. It's a feeling we all know.

But remember, when it comes along...
it's always sure to go.

And sometimes, if you're lucky (I promise this is true),

the Fear that you are frightened of...

is more afraid of you.

# Reader's Note
## by Tammy L. Hughes, PhD

Reading **The Fears You Fear** can help children to identify and manage their experiences of fear. Helping children to identify and sort thoughts (which happen in your mind), feelings like fear (which happen in your body), and actions (things you do) helps them to develop early awareness about themselves and others. As children age, this is a book that can be revisited to illustrate how the mind and body are connected and how their thinking can impact or change their feelings. As children mature, they develop the ability to control their behavior by regulating their thoughts and feelings. This book provides a lighthearted way to start these discussions with young minds.

## What Is Fear?

Fear is an unpleasant emotion that is caused by danger. It is universal and involuntary. It is a basic emotion that we are *born* with—even though we can be afraid of different things. Indeed, children's fears are often determined by family or cultural experiences. Fears change as children age.

Fear is supposed to be a brief warning signal telling us to pay attention because danger is ahead. This is illustrated in the story, for example, by the "beeping cars on busy roads." You may ask your child what we should say to make sure the little girl in the picture doesn't walk into the street. "Stop!" they are likely to reply (or you can prompt them). It is not simply the word *stop*, but rather the urgent tone indicating this is a serious nonnegotiable command; the tone conveys the warning. Ensuring a child's safety is an appropriate use of the fear signal.

However, sometimes we experience fear when there is no danger. Fear of the dark is one of the most common fears in children and adolescents. Decreased visibility allows the mind to wonder and increases feelings of vulnerability. When fear takes over, small sounds can be interpreted as large monsters. Although there are many ways to help children manage nighttime fears, choosing books that specifically address a fear of the dark has proven to be an effective technique.

## Recognizing and Managing Fears

Younger children can have difficulty accurately interpreting emotions that are felt in the body—as every parent of a tired and hungry child insisting that they aren't tired or hungry knows. Helping children to accurately connect the emotion they are experiencing and physical sensations in their body is an essential step towards developing emotion awareness, a building block that is required for emotional control.

Children will notice their fear when they, or someone else, start to breathe fast, their heart beats louder, or they sweat or shiver. When that happens, taming fears is about focusing on managing those physical responses. This helps to calm the sympathetic nervous system that was activated by the emotion. Here are some strategies that can help:

- Take slow, deep breaths.
- Count to ten.
- Provide a comfort item like a stuffed toy to allow your child to reassure themselves.
- Use night lights or dim hallway lights for nighttime.
- Teach your child to talk back to fears by saying something like "that's not real."

It is not advisable to give in to the fear by, for example, letting children sleep in bed with you or keeping the lights on all night. Avoiding the situations they find fearful will only strengthen the fear response.

It is possible to misinterpret feelings, as shown in the story when fear "is excitement in disguise." This also illustrates that the way you think about a feeling can change how you experience it. One of the critical lessons from this book is that fears, and feelings, come and go. It is important to reassure children that fearful feelings will pass.

Fear is good because it can help us. The goal, as with all our emotions, is not to get rid of fears or avoid them, but rather to understand and process them. It is only when fears are persistently unwarranted or unrelenting that there should be concern. If your child's fears interfere with daily life, it may be advisable to consult a mental health professional.

**Tammy L. Hughes, PhD, ABPP** is a school psychologist, licensed psychologist and board certified in school psychology, and a professor at Duquesne University in Pittsburgh, PA.